In the name of Allāh, the B

The Broken Bead

Reflections on the Life of Hazrat Fatima (AS)

By

Ayatullah al-ᶜUẓmā Shaykh Ḥusayn Vaḥīd Khorasānī

Translated By

Ali Raza Rizvi

Published by The Saviour Foundation

Published by The Saviour Foundation

www.thesaviour.org.uk

Foreword

The Queen of the Ladies of the Universe, Fāṭima (AS), the daughter of the Seal of the Prophets, Muḥammad (SA), is the symbol of infallibility. She embodies courage for all men and women who stand against tyranny and oppression. She is the first female in Islām who stood up in defence of the guardianship [*wilāyat*]. She is the backbone of the movement of the Commander of the Faithful (AS). If it were not for her and her children, then Islām would have been orphaned for eternity.

Born from the noblest parents, Prophet Muḥammad (SA) and Khadīja (AS), she truly understood what nobility meant. Her trained servants became the best practising people in society. Her children touched the peaks of human perfection. Her husband deemed her a support in obeying God. Her father regarded her not only as his daughter, but as his mother as well. He showed his respect for her by standing up for her when she entered his assembly.

History regards her as the most eloquent female in Arabic. Her status in knowledge was so high that the highest-ranking companions of the Messenger of Allāh would come and learn from her. Pleasing her was pleasing her father, and pleasing her father meant pleasing Allāh. Thus, the true believers always wished to please her.

She was born on the 20th of Jamādī al-Thānī in the fifth year of Biʿthat (five years after the Prophet's proclamation of prophethood). On her birth she bore witness that, "There is no god but Allāh and my father is the Messenger of Allāh."

She lived with both her parents until the death of her mother when she was only seven years old. When her father migrated to Medina, she followed him. In Medina, her father received many proposals for her hand in marriage. He accepted the proposal of his cousin ᶜAlī ibn Abū Ṭālib (AS). Fāṭima (AS) married ᶜAlī (AS) on the first of Dhil Ḥijja in the second year of migration. In their fruitful marriage, Fāṭima (AS) gave birth to two sons, Ḥasan and Ḥusayn (AS), and two daughters, Zaynab and Umm Kulthūm (AS). Her third son, who was miscarried, was named Muḥsin (AS) by the Holy Prophet (SA).

During her life in Medina, the women of Medina would come to her house and learn from her. She has narrated many traditions from her father. Many of these have been reported from her husband, ᶜAlī ibn Abū Ṭālib (AS). Other reports are from her children. Some traditions are also reported from some noble companions who she taught. Her style of teaching, speaking, way of walking, and appearance most resembled her father (SA). She was the most beloved person to her father, the Messenger of Allāh (SA). Likewise, she loved the Prophet the most.

She was greatly saddened after the death of her father. One of the reasons for her grief was the sad demise of her father. Other reasons for her anguish were the denial of her inheritance and the usurping of the rights of her husband by the government. As a consequence of the mental and physical torture she received from the people in her era, she suddenly left this world when only about nineteen. Her martyrdom occurred either 75 or 95 days after the death of her father. Therefore, she died on the 13th of Jamādī al-Awwal or the 3rd of Jamādī al-Thānī in 11 Hijra.

This book contains some lectures on the status of Fāṭima (AS) delivered on the day of her martyrdom. These lectures were delivered by one of the leading figures of the Religious Seminary in Qum. The city of Qum has the largest Shīᶜite religious seminary, containing over sixty thousand students and researchers. The highest level in the traditional Shīᶜite Uṣūlī Seminary is the level of *Khārij*. In Qum, the most popular teacher of *Khārij* in terms of attendance and material, is the Grand Ayatullāh Shaykh Ḥusayn Vaḥīd Khorāsānī (may Allāh protect him). His works, especially on the lives of the Infallibles (AS), are unique not only in eloquence and style, but also in depth and innovativeness. The Ayatullāh elaborates upon aspects of their holy lives which the reader may never have discovered before. His words leave a spiritual mark upon the reader, and add to his recognition of the Holy Progeny (AS). The Ayatullāh is especially attached to Haḍrat Fātima and Imam al-Sadiq (AS).

Today there are numerous books about the brief life of Fāṭima (AS) in this world. In fact, encyclopaedias are being compiled on her life and contribution. These encyclopaedias differ in size; some are as little as one or two volumes. Others are six to seven volumes; however, some are as vast as ten or twenty volumes. Nevertheless, may Allah accept this humble effort of just a few pages to please her, *āmīn.*

Ali Raza Rizvi
London, England

In the Name of Allāh, the Beneficent, the Merciful

All Praise be to Allāh, the Lord of the Worlds. Blessings of Allāh be upon our Master Muhammad and his Purified Progeny, in particular the remaining one on earth. Curse be upon their enemies till the Day of Judgement.

The purpose of creation is to recognise and serve the Exalted Lord; however, this recognition is not possible without the path of revelation. The light of intellect is extinguished before the light of His Reverence and Pride. Generating and forming ideas about the essence, attributes and actions of the Unseen of all Unseen is darkness upon darkness. *Whatever you have differentiated with your imagination in the finest of concepts is a creation created like yourselves, which returns to you.*[1] The light to reach the path is: *Allāh is the Light of the heavens and the earth.*[2] This is confined to the niche of the heart, in which the lamp of revelation is lit: *(This is) a Book which We have revealed unto you so that you may bring people forth from utter darkness into light by their Lord's permission.*[3]

The service is worthy of the Most Praised and the Most Holy who created the human being from a uniting life-germ, the human being who is the heart of this world even though he did not have a mention of his name in this universe. Allāh bestowed man with hearing so that he can give ear to the verses of His law, and gave him sight so that he may see the verses of wisdom. Although He created this creation from despicable fluid, it reached the level of wisdom, certainty, knowledge of certainty, vision of certitude, and true certainty. *So praised be Allāh, the Best of Creators.*[4]

However, worship of that Unique Being, just like His recognition, is not possible except with the constitution of worship legislated from the Most High, the Most Great, and delivered by His great prophets. This is so that everyone can call the Lord of

Glory and Honour with His names of Exaltation and Glory, which are the gems from treasures of His cognition. *To Allāh alone belong all the most Beautiful Names; so call unto Him thereby.*[5]

The recognition and worship, which is the purpose of the creation of the mankind and the result of sending the prophets, has reached its completion with the sending of the Seal of the Prophets (SA), who is the Seal of what has happened and the Opener to what will happen.

The noble tree of religion, which Allāh the Exalted has planted in the land of nature with pure wisdom and power: *So set your face uprightly for religion, in natural devotion to the truth, the nature caused by Allāh in which He has made people.*[6] He showed the king of its fruits on the Day of revelation of this verse: *This day have I perfected your religion for you, completed My favour upon you, and chosen Islam as your religion.*[7] And whatever was possible of the teachings of guidance was combined in the City of Knowledge and Seal of Wisdom. Allāh, the Exalted, confined that City of Knowledge with conclusive wisdom so error and desire cannot enter it. He guarded it from flawed intellects and corrupt hearts so that they cannot damage the gems of knowledge and wisdom with mistakes and desires. He opened only one route to that City and that is the Straight Path of the Greatest Guardianship. He opened simply one door to the world and mankind, which is the door of the highest level of Imāmat that requires definite infallibility from all mistakes and desires. He (SA) said: *I am the City of Knowledge and ᶜAlī is its Gate.*[8]

It is noteworthy that the link between the whole of the *Ummah* with the highest Messenger (AS) and the greatest Imām is the human *ḥūrī* Fāṭima al-Zahrā' (AS), till the Day of Judgement.

It is she who is the means of continuation in this world for the essence of the Seal of the Prophets (SA). The dimension of his sovereignty, which is his progeny and the dimension of his divinity, which is his religion, have both remained through the greatest truthful lady, Fāṭima (AS).

It is she who is the means of the rising of the stars of Imāmat. The horizon of her life is the rising of the forbearance of Ḥasan (AS), the bravery of Ḥusayn (AS), the worship of Sajjād (AS), the nobility of Bāqir (AS), the traditions of Jaᶜfar (AS), the knowledge of Kāẓim (AS), the proofs of Riḍā (AS), the generosity of Taqī (AS), the purity of Naqī (AS), and the dignity of ᶜAskarī (AS). From Ḥusayn (AS), who is the lamp of guidance and arch of salvation, to the Promised Mahdī (AS), with whom end the legacies of the prophets, and due to whom mankind is given sustenance. Because of his existence the earth and the heaven remain. They are the fruits of *the noble tree, whose root is firm and whose branches are in heaven, yielding its fruit in every season by the permission of its Lord.*[9]

In short, the gems of the hidden treasures of the Exalted Lord are from the pearl of infallibility. The glowing torch (SA) of His Prophets, from Adam to the Last One, and the shining lamp of the Imāmat of the Guided Imāms (AS) are radiant due to the essence of Fāṭima al-Zahrā' (AS). The last pearl of this treasure and the shining star of this sky is he *who will fill the earth with peace and justice like it was filled with injustice and oppression,*[10] and due to his existence is the interpretation of this verse: *He it is Who sent His Messenger with guidance and the religion of truth, that He might cause it to prevail over all religions, though the polytheists may be averse.*[11] Due to him is the explanation of this verse: *And the earth shall beam with the light of its Lord.*[12]

It must be known that the rank of the Night of Destiny, which is the place of the greatest book of Allāh, is unknown. The position of *Kawthar*, which is a gift of the Lord of the greatest throne to the Noble Messenger, is concealed from our perception.

The Shīᶜahs and the Sunnīs have both acknowledged the issuance of these words from the tongue of a prophet (SA) *who does not speak out of desire.*[13] The critics, who have spent all of their abilities trying to weaken the transmission of the traditions in the merits of the infallible household (of the Prophet (SA)), are unable to alter the transmission of this tradition. They also bore witness with content and the conditions of the experts of tradition that the Messenger of Allāh (SA) has said: *Indeed, Fāṭima is a part of me. Whatever distresses her distresses me and whatever hurts her hurts me.*[14] And he (SA) has also said: *Fāṭima is a part of me. Whoever angers her has angered me.*[15] He has expressed Fāṭima (AS) to be a part of his essence.

The one, who is the first to be created[16] and the best who ever uttered, has declared her to be a part of his essence. The one, who is the greatest name from the beautiful names of Allāh and the highest attribute of Allāh from the attributes, has declared her anger to be his own. His anger is the anger of Allāh. This status indicates that Fāṭima (AS) is a branch from the attribute of Allāh's light. The reflection of the anger of Allāh and the Messenger is in the anger of the most truthful Lady. Hence, both of the sects have narrated about Fāṭima (AS), *Indeed, Allāh is angered for your anger, and becomes pleased with your pleasure.*[17]

The highest level of human perfection is infallibility, where pleasure and anger rotate around the pleasure and anger of God. However, the upper level of infallibility is when the perfect human being reaches a stage where his pleasure is absolutely for the pleasure of God and his anger is totally for the anger of God. Fāṭima al-Zahrā' (AS) is one for whose pleasure Allāh is pleased, and for whose anger Allāh is angered. This is a status which causes (even) the perfect ones to be astonished.

She is the one where the stars of the sky of guardianship shine and she is the one where the mysteries of the limits of the

Book of Guidance are treasured. She is the one who is the spouse of one and mother of eleven (altogether 12) Imāms from the progeny of Ismāᶜīl (AS), about whom God informed Ibrāhīm (AS) in book 17 of Torah. She is the one who is a great sign that appeared in the states of enlightenment of John [Yūḥannā]; a lady that raised the sun, the moon was beneath her feet and on her head was a crown with twelve stars.[18]

In the chapter "the Smoke" from the Qur'ān, she is 'the Blessed Night' *therein every wise affair is made distinct.*[19] She is the one in the Noble Qur'ān, who has been regarded as plural while being singular; *our women.*[20] She and her husband are the two oceans of Prophethood and Knowledge that have been interpreted from: *He has made the two seas to flow freely (so that) they meet together.*[21] She is the only woman whose prayer the Almighty God has paralleled with the prayer of the Last of the Messengers (SA) and the Master of the Successors (AS).

She is the solitary lady who has been placed with the crown of the verse: *We only feed you for Allāh's sake; we desire from you neither reward nor thanks.*[22]

The Messenger of Allāh (SA) saw that it was written on the Door of Paradise in the Night of Ascension: *Fāṭima is the chosen one of Allāh.*[23] Indeed, it is Aḥmad who is free to choose, who is worthy of a daughter who is the chosen one of Allāh.

She is the one about whom the Messenger of Allāh (SA) has said: *I will be resurrected on a horse-like animal made of light, whose step will be as far as he can see, while Fāṭima will be resurrected before me.*[24] It is sufficient for her that she will be resurrected before the Leader of the First and the Last. This is the manifestation of the verse: *On that day you will see the faithful men and the faithful women—their light running before them.*[25] She will be resurrected before the light of he who Allāh has named the Glowing Torch in the Noble Qur'ān and the Verse of Light; He has announced him as the likeness of His own light.

It is enough to describe her personality as the first to enter *in the seat of honour with a most Powerful King.*[26] On the other hand, *the first person to enter Paradise is Fāṭima (AS).*[27] When she takes the Abode of Mercy, the prophets (AS) will come to visit her; *Adam and all the other Prophets (AS) will visit you.*[28]

The Prophet (SA) is the only being for whom Allāh has said to the believers that 'I conferred': *Certainly Allāh conferred a benefit upon the believers when He raised among them a Messenger from among themselves.*[29] However, as a persistence of his essence, Allāh has conferred to the Prophet his daughter as a benefit: *Verily We have given you Kawthar. So pray to your Lord and offer sacrifice. Verily your enemy shall be the one who is cut off (in progeny).*[30]

The treasures of the knowledge of the Infallible Imāms (AS) are summarised into three books after the Holy Qur'ān: *Jafr*, *Jāmiᶜah* and *Muṣḥaf Fāṭima* (AS). After the death of the Messenger of Allāh (SA), Fāṭima (AS) became extremely grieved from the separation of her father. Based on the authentic tradition from the sixth Imām, Jaᶜfar ibn Muhammad al-Ṣādiq (AS), Jibr'īl used to descend to her presence to console her and would inform her of her father's position. He would also inform her of what would happen to her progeny after her. The Commander of the Faithful (AS) would write down everything. That scripture [*Muṣḥaf*] became the treasure of knowledge of what was going to happen.

The influence of her holy soul and the magnetism that was in her must be realised, the part of the reality of Muhammad, that the Lord of Mighty Power, from the highest part of the horizon, and Jibr'īl, from the farthest lote-tree, would be subdued to her influence and magnetised to her reality. Indeed, peace and protection from the filth of the materialistic world caused the angels and archangel to descend for the Night of Destiny, who is the dawn of the suns of the sky of Guardianship.

It has come in an authentic tradition from Mūsa ibn Qāsim, who says that I asked Abū Jaᶜfar, the second, (Imām Taqī

(AS)), "I intended to perform the circumambulation of the House of God (Makkah) on your behalf and on behalf of your father. I was told that it is not permissible to do so on behalf of the successors (of the Prophet)."

He (AS) replied: *Whatever is possible for you in performing the circumambulation on their behalf, do it.*

After three years, I had the chance to visit him again; therefore, I told him, "One day I performed the circumambulation on behalf of the Messenger of Allāh (SA) three times. The Imām (AS) said three times, 'May Allāh bless the Messenger of Allāh.' The next day I performed it on behalf of the Commander of the Faithful (AS), the third day on behalf of Ḥasan (AS), the fourth day on behalf of Ḥusayn (AS), the fifth day on behalf of ᶜAlī ibn al-Ḥusayn (AS), on the sixth day on behalf of Abū Jaᶜfar Muhammad ibn ᶜAlī (AS), the seventh day on behalf of Jaᶜfar ibn Muhammad (AS), the eighth day on behalf of your grandfather Mūsa (AS), the ninth day on behalf of your father ᶜAlī (AS) and on the tenth day on your behalf. O my master, I sometimes perform the circumambulation on behalf of your grandmother, Fāṭima (AS), and sometimes I do not."

He (AS) responded: *Do perform this circumambulation more often, for it is the most rewarding of the actions you perform.*[31]

The ocean of merits of one whose name makes the circumambulation of the House of Allāh the most rewarding action cannot be described in speech or writing.

Shaykh Ṣadūq has mentioned a tradition in his books; *al-Amālī*, *ᶜIlal al-Sharāyiᶜ* and *al-Khiṣāl*, from Imām al-Ṣādiq (AS): *Fāṭima (AS) has nine names before Allāh, the Mighty and High: Fāṭima, Ṣiddīqah, Mubārakah, Ṭāhirah, Zakiyyah, Rāḍiyah, Marḍiyyah, Muḥaddathah and Zahrā'..." towards the end of the tradition he (AS) added, "If the Commander of the Faithful (AS) had not married her, then there was no one parallel to her on the surface of the earth till the Day of Judgement; not Adam or anyone after him.*[32]

The names which were given to her from Allāh, the Mighty and High, each indicate a status and rank which cannot be explained in this brief work. It would suffice with the mention of two traditions regarding the first and the last names. It is narrated from the sixth Imām (AS) in the commentary of the chapter of the Qur'ān "the Destiny" that he said: *The Night of Destiny is Fāṭima. Therefore, whoever recognises Fāṭima in her true recognition has comprehended the Night of Destiny. Indeed, she was named Fāṭima because no creation is capable of recognising her.*[33]

Shaykh Ṣadūq has mentioned a tradition in his books; *ᶜIlal al-Sharāyiᶜ* and *Maᶜānī al-Akhbār*, on the authority of ᶜAmmāra that he said, "I asked a question from Abū ᶜAbd Allāh (al-Ṣādiq (AS)), 'Why was Fāṭima (AS) named al-Zahrā'?" He (AS) answered: *She was named so because when she used to stand up for prayer, her light would shine for the inhabitants of the heavens like the lights of the stars for the inhabitants of the earth.*[34]

The extent of the light of her knowledge and faith is so intense that its rising reaches the inhabitants of the highest levels. The Imām (AS) was asked in another tradition why Fāṭima (AS) was named al-Zahrā', he replied: *For, there is a dome for her in Paradise made of red rubies, the height of which is the travel of one year. It is hanging with the power of the Almighty. It is neither connected to anything from above, nor does it have any pillars below it. It has a thousand doors and at each door there are a thousand angels. The inhabitants of the Paradise see it like you all see the most shining star in the horizon of the sky.*[35]

Based on the judgement of the intellect, the Qur'ān and the Sunnah, the levels in the world of reward are according to the levels of knowledge, faith, ethical conduct and good deeds. The distance between the dome, which is the place of Fāṭima (AS), and the place of the inhabitants of the Paradise explains the difference between the status of the inhabitants of the Paradise and the status of Fāṭima (AS). That difference is like the difference of the sky to the earth.

Quṭb al-Dīn narrates from the Sixth Imām (AS): *When Khadīja (AS) passed away, Fāṭima (AS) would come to the Messenger of Allāh (SA) and ask, 'Where is my mother, O Messenger of Allāh?' The Messenger of Allāh would not answer her (due to sadness). Jibra'īl came down and said, 'Your Lord commands you to say 'peace' to Fāṭima (AS) and tell her, your mother is with Āsiyah and Maryam (AS) in a palace, the roof of which is made of gold and its pillars are of ruby.' Therefore, Fāṭima (AS) said, 'Indeed Allāh is peace, from Him is peace and to Him is peace.'*[36]

The pen and the words are incapable of writing the status of someone to whom the Seal of the Prophets (SA) is commanded to deliver peace from God when she was only a child, and the trustworthy Jibra'īl carries the condolences from the Lord of the worlds to her.

Her Godly soul transformed the hearts of the ones who had the honour of serving her vicinity, so much so that their accepted prayers ruled the laws of nature. The power of their intent from the lowest part of the earth subjugated the worlds beyond heavens.

Ibn Shahr Āshūb narrates a tradition from ᶜAlī ibn Muᶜammar, who said, "After the death of Fāṭima (AS), Umm Ayman could not bear the emptiness of Medina from the Most Truthful Lady. So she travelled to Makkah. In Juḥfah, she became so thirsty that she thought she was going to die of thirst. She lifted her head to the heavens and said, 'O Lord, I am the servant of the daughter of Your Messenger.' A utensil full of water from Paradise came for her. She drank from it and after that for seven years she did not feel hunger or thirst."[37]

In the same book it is narrated from Mālik ibn Dīnār that he said, "When people were preparing for the pilgrimage of Hajj, I saw a lady who people were advising to avoid the travel for Hajj due to her weakness, but she did not accept. In the middle of nowhere her camel stopped from going further. The weak lady lifted her head to the sky and said, 'Neither You made me stay in my house, nor did You take me to Your House. If someone other than You had done this to me, then I would have complained against him to You.' Suddenly, a man appeared in that desert. He was holding the bridle of a camel. He said to the woman, 'Ride this.' When she rode it, the camel crossed that desert like lightning. When I reached the place of circumambulation, I saw the woman there. I said, 'For the sake of God, tell me who you are!' She replied, 'I am Shuhra daughter of Maska, who was the daughter of Fiḍḍa the servant of al-Zahrā'.'"[38]

One whose heart is the throne of the Beneficent in recognition of Allāh, whose intent is perished in the intent of Allāh, and whose swollen feet in the place of worship are a witness of the worship of Allāh, then the reward of serving such a person is acceptance of prayer in the presence of the Lord of all Lords.

The dinner table used to come down from heaven for Maryam, the most truthful woman of her time. Similarly, water comes down from the heaven for the servant of the most truthful woman of all times. If Āṣif ibn Barkhiyā shortens the earth with the power of some knowledge of the Book, then the granddaughter of Fiḍḍa, servant of Fāṭima (AS) travels through the mountains and deserts like lightning.

The Day of Judgement is the Day of accountability and reward. It is a day for which it said: *And We will set up a just balance on the Day of Resurrection, so no soul shall be dealt with unjustly in the least;*[39] *and the measuring out on that day will be just.*[40] It will be a day of righteousness and justice in its full term. The actions and levels of closeness (to Allāh) will be based on the levels of knowledge and faith. *Allāh will exalt those of you who believe, and those who are given knowledge, in high degrees;*[41] *and for all are degrees according to what they did.*[42] It is a day on which the abasing and exalting, rising and reducing will be based on the quantity and quality of thoughts, ethics and deeds. *When the great event comes to pass, there is no belying its coming to pass—abasing (one party), exalting (the other).*[43] The resurrection of everyone is according to his character. *On that day men shall come forth in sundry bodies that they may be shown their works. So, he who has done an atom's weight of good shall see it and he who has done an atom's weight of evil shall see it.*[44]

On such a day, the endless mercies of the Bestowing God and disobedience and sins of mankind will be reached out to. Due to the absolute mercy of the All-Merciful Lord, mankind, who did not exist, was created with limbs and parts of the body in the darkness and hidden womb from a very lowly life-germ. The world is still astonished at the mystery of his creation, from his systems of sight and hearing, to his reaching the high levels of wisdom and knowledge that have dissected the atom and have discovered the furthest of the galaxies. *There surely came over man a period of time when he was a thing not worth mentioning. Surely We have created man from a small life-germ uniting (itself): We mean to try him, so We have made him hearing, seeing. Surely We have shown him the way, be he grateful or ungrateful.*[45] *And He has made subservient to you whatsoever is in the heavens and whatsoever is in the earth.*[46]

Every moment of mankind's life is not only related to the earth; rather, it is related to the solar system, and the solar system is connected to the galaxy, and the galaxy to the Milky Way. *And if you count Allāh's favours, you will not be able to number them.*[47] Therefore, each and every act of disobedience to Allāh is being unthankful to His countless favours. It is also belittling His reverence, His eternal Majesty and His endless Exaltation and Glory. On the other hand, each and every act of obedience is a favour in itself, which causes a human being to be included in the mercy of the Lord. It is achieved through His favour and bounty. Hence, it necessitates thanking. There is no end or limit to this cycle. In conclusion, the wise and the mystics see nothing but fault and blame in the presence of the Bestowing God. *Verily, Allāh is feared only by those of His servants who are endowed with knowledge.*[48]

In obtaining such mercies with such errors, the only path of salvation is access [*tawassul*] and attainment of intercession of one who has reached the highest possible status of absolute service (to Allāh). He must be at the stage where Allāh says: *Who is he that can intercede with Him but by His permission?*[49] These are the ones who have eliminated their pleasure and anger in the pleasure and anger of God. They are the ones who, in place of their evil desires, have placed His divine intent as their sovereign. Their status is that the intent of the Lord, in the decrees of His affairs, comes down to them and is executed from their House.

We suffice with an authentic tradition in this place, which is transmitted from the Great Shaykh Muhammad ibn Nuᶜmān Mufīd, on the authority of Shaykh Ṣadūq, Muhammad ibn ᶜAlī ibn Mūsa, on the authority of ᶜAlī ibn Ibrāhīm, on the authority of his father Ibrāhīm ibn Hāshim, on the authority of Muhammad ibn Abū ᶜUmayr, on the authority of Ābān ibn ᶜUthmān, on the authority of Imām Jaᶜfar ibn Muhammad al-Ṣādiq (AS).[50]

This tradition is most authentic, as it contains in its transmission Shaykh Mufīd, Shaykh Ṣadūq, ᶜAlī ibn Ibrāhīm and Ibrāhīm ibn Hāshim, who are the greatest of the trustworthy and just, and pillars of knowledge and traditions. It also contains two people from the narrators on whom there is consensus in the Imāmīs, that if anything comes from them then the tradition is authentic.

A part of this tradition is related to this topic, wherein Abū ᶜAbd Allāh al-Ṣādiq (AS) said: *On the Day of Resurrection, Allāh will gather all the people in one place. At that time, an angel will call out, 'close your eyes and lower your heads until Faṭima, daughter of Muhammad (SA), crosses the Ṣirāṭ.'*

All will close their eyes and bow their heads while Faṭima (AS) comes riding on a she-camel from the camels of the Paradise. Seventy thousand angels will be accompanying her. She will stop at an honourable place from the places of the Day of Judgement. She will then come off the camel and will hold the shirt with the blood stains of Ḥusayn ibn ᶜAlī (AS) and will say: O Lord! This is the shirt of my son and You know how my son was treated.

At that point Allāh, the Mighty and High, will say to Faṭima: I desire your pleasure.

In every sentence of this noble tradition, there are mysteries. The shirt she will hold in her hand is connected to the revenge of Allāh, which the Messenger of Allāh (SA) placed on the pole of the Throne, and the pole will tremble till the Day of Judgement.[51]

According to the tradition which Shaykh Ṣadūq has counted as the most authentic of traditions in the chapter of pilgrimage [*ziyārah*] in his book *Man Lā Yaḥḍuruhu al-Faqīh*, it says: *All shadowed things of the Throne and the spirits of all creations trembled for that blood (of Ḥusayn (AS)). All those which can be seen and all those that cannot be seen shed tears for that blood.*[52] The blood, which at the time of being shed with its dry lips and witnessing of pain said: *In the name of Allāh, for Allāh and for the people of the Messenger of Allāh.*[53]

The price of such a pearl is nothing but that the Exalted will call him and will guarantee him His pleasure on the Day of Judgement. This pleasure will suffice for the intercession of the sinful ones of their sins from this *Ummah*.

She is the one whose father is a mercy for the universe and whose son is the lamp of light of guidance. He is Allāh's vast mercy and the gate of salvation for the *Ummah*. She is the Honour of God herself and is the continuation of the essence of the last message till the Day of Judgement. She can open the doors of mercy for the *Ummah* on such a day of yearning with manifestation of her service, earnestness and sincerity.

The illuminations of perfection and lights of magnificence of such a bright sun on the horizon of infallibility is more than which can be handled with partial intellects. My intention was to give an indication as a reminder for the wise.

What happened after the Messenger of Allāh (AS), that such a personality, who possessed a delicate heart, tore her heart away from sons like Ḥasan and Ḥusayn (AS), lowered her eyes from her little daughters and said: *O My God! Hasten my death to me!*[54] She also said: *So many calamities were poured on me that if they were poured on days they would change into nights.*[55] When she was placed in her grave, her afflicted body had remained like a shadow: *She had become like a shadow.*[56]

ᶜAlī (AS), the man whose power of determination made both worlds bend over knees, had become so moved with this tribulation that he said to the Messenger of Allāh (SA): *As to my grief, it knows no bounds, and as to my nights, they will remain sleepless.*[57]

She was such a pearl that was the apple of the eye of the universe and mankind, but was afflicted in such a way that the Commander of the Faithful (AS) addressed the Prophet (SA) saying: *Your daughter will soon inform you of the atrocities against her.*[58] She was buried unfortunately during the night and no one knew what she was, what she bore and what she went through. It was such that the bravest man (ᶜAlī (AS)) had to say in the sermon called *Shiqshiqiyyah*: *I adopted patience although there was pricking in the eye and suffocation in the throat.* He lived for thirty years with suffocation and pricking in his eye; yet, he remained patient. A patience which did not tremble his feet in the Battle of Uḥud; likewise, in the Battle of Khaybar he showed his courageousness. What is more, in eighty other places he broke all barriers. However, upon the death of Fāṭima (AS) he said: *O Messenger of Allāh, my patience about your chosen (daughter) has been exhausted.*[59]

Our existence and the perfection of our essence are due to the Noble Messenger (SA). He is the means of our constitutional [*takwīniyyah*] and legislative [*tashrīʿiyyah*] nurture from the Lord of the Worlds. He has an eternal right over every Muslim due to the guidance he has given about the Beginning (God) and the End in whoever Allāh sent and whatever He sent. Based on the demand of wisdom in thanking the Benefactor and the Islamic ruling in necessity of love for the Near Relatives: *Say: I do not ask of you any reward for it but love for my near relatives.*[60]

Fāṭima (AS) is the most beloved and nearest relative of the Messenger of Allāh (SA). The nightly burial and concealment of her grave was a tragic event, for, she is the treasure of God's mysteries, the Honour of God, the part of the Seal of the Messengers, the wife of the Master of the Successors, and the mother of the Imāms (AS). Our responsibility is that we should rise and do whatever is possible in reverence for the signs of the day of her martyrdom. Only because the day of her martyrdom is the certification of proving the righteousness of the first of the oppressed, "I have not seen any right like his being shattered."[61]

Revival of the martyrdom day of Fāṭima (AS) is revival of the Commander of the Faithful (AS). Revival of his affair is the revival of the affair of the Seal of the Prophets (SA), as he is the soul of the Prophet. Hence, the revival of the Seal of the Prophets (SA) is revival of all the prophets and apostles. Thus, the revival of the prophets of Allāh is the revival of recognition and service to the Lord of the Worlds.

With the order of this verse in seeking access: *O you who believe! Fear Allāh and seek access to Him;*[62] the best deed, which is pleasure of Allāh, His Messenger and His sent Imāms, is to revere the signs of grief for her.

I hope that the ones that have hope in the intercession of her father on the Day of Judgement, wish to see her husband at the time of death, and desire to be counted in the prayer of the Most Truthful Lady in the fright and loneliness of the first night of the grave, will struggle within the limits and in accordance of her status to carry out the commemoration of her martyrdom. All religious organisations should raise banners in commemoration of the Mother of Noble Imāms (AS), paying condolences to the *Sibṭ Akbar* (Ḥasan) and the Master of the Martyrs (AS), with the hope that we may be paying our homage to her father and her husband, who are the first and second persons of all possible beings. We must also commemorate with the hope that it may be an ointment over the wounds of her infallible sons, who are the divine leaders of the men and the jinn. It should also be a means of showing our respect for the one who is the Anchor of the earth and the heavens, the Guardian of the Time and the Master of the Age.

It is necessary for all believers to pay attention to this point, not through prejudice and force, but because reasoning and proof demand: *Surely the (true) religion with Allāh is Islam;*[63] also because Islam is firm in its principles and practices due to the Infallible Imāms: *Through us Allāh was recognised and through us Allāh was served. We are the guides to Allāh. If we were not there, then Allāh would not have been served.*[64] There are hands which are working in weakening the strong connection of our people with the divine leaders, who are the light of guidance and the ark of salvation of the *Ummah*. They want us to turn away from the Right Path, which is the fruit of the lives of the Infallible Imāms (AS), and is the result of the scientific and practical struggle of Godly scholars and guided jurists, to a confirmed misguidance, which is deviation from the guardianship of Allāh's Guardians and immunity from His enemies. Therefore, our intellectual and Islamic responsibility is to revere the signs of our religion. The most apparent implication of this is to show respect to the Most Truthful Lady (AS), to hold on to the Rope of Allāh, which are the Qur'ān and the Progeny (of the Prophet), and to safeguard the path of Allāh from the thieves.

Fortunate are those who are successful in serving the holy cause of the one who will intercede on the Day of Resurrection and acquire the pleasure of Allāh through her pleasure. For, the pleasure of Allāh is the end hope of all the Prophets and Guardians: *This is Allāh's blessing, He gives it to whom He pleases.*[65] It is a must that through establishing the signs on the day of her martyrdom, this true practice is safeguarded from the deception of the enemies and hypocrites.

For blessing, I conclude my words with the last will of that Holy Lady (AS):

In the name of Allāh, the Beneficent, the Merciful. This is the will which Fāṭima (AS), daughter of the Messenger of Allāh (SA) has made. She bears witness that there is no god but Allāh and that Muhammad is His Servant and Messenger. She bears witness that Paradise is true, Hell-fire is true and the Day of Judgement is to come, there is no doubt in it and that Allāh will raise the dead from the graves. O ᶜAlī! I am Fāṭima, daughter of Muhammad. Allāh married me to you so that I can be for you both in this world and the Hereafter. You have more right over me than myself. Give me Ḥunūṭ[1] *yourself, wash my body and shroud me during the night. Pray on my body and bury me during the night. Do not inform anyone of my death. I commend you to Allāh's protection. Deliver my greetings [*salām*] to all of my progeny till the Day of Judgement.*[66]

This is a will which the one making it made it at the time of witnessing the Beginning, the End, Paradise, Hell, the Messengership, and the Messenger. From the time of the revelation of the verse: *Allāh bears witness that there is no god but He, and (so do) the angels and those possessed of knowledge, maintaining His creation with justice; there is no god but He, the Mighty, the Wise,*[67] till the Day of the Witnesses, such a witness from a martyr has never been established before, nor shall ever be established after.

This is a witness that was established in the presence of two witnesses: the first being Allāh and second His Guardian, *Say:*

---

[1] Rubbing of camphor over seven parts of prostration.

Allāh is sufficient as a witness between me and you and whoever has knowledge of the Book.[68]

The recognition of this witness, its bearer, and what it bears upon is specified with the ones with knowledge, who know the levels of the Unity of God, the status of the Seal of the Messengers, the reality of Paradise and Hell, and the mysteries of the raising of the dead from their graves and the difficulties of the Day of Reckoning.

Our intention is to signify the last sentence of this will: 'Deliver my greetings to all of my progeny till the Day of Judgement.' This sentence is in itself a witness upon the fact that she (AS) knew, through connection with the unseen world and encompassment over the world beyond sight [*shuhūd*], that her progeny will continue till the Day of Judgement. She asked the Commander of the Faithful (AS) to deliver her greetings to all her children till the Day of Judgement.

The Fāṭimid men and women must realise what a crown she has placed over their heads. They must also understand what immense responsibility she has laid over their shoulders. What position does the crown of the kings of this world hold in comparison with the metaphorical crown of the greeting from the Honour of God to her progeny? The greeting of the Most Truthful Woman (AS) has risen from the Heart of the Qur'ān, the chapter of Yāsīn, which is connected to the greeting from the Heart of the Chapter of Yāsīn: *Peace: a word from a Merciful Lord.*[69]

An enormous accountability is placed in the answer to this greeting. This greeting is from a sacred personality to whom God Himself sends blessings and salutations: *He is Allāh, besides Whom there is no god; the King, the Holy, the Giver of peace.*[70]

The reply to this greeting [*salām*] is that all of her children should defend the rights of their mother up to the Day of

Judgement. The reply to this greeting is according to the (spiritual) status of every Sayyid.[2]

It must not happen that a Sayyid reaches a position where he comes short of his duty towards proving her righteousness. For indeed proving her righteousness is reviving the affair of the divine leadership of the Imāms, because she used to say to her father with an afflicted body: *My strength has finished.*[71] She used to say in the grief of her father: *He, who smells the fragrance from the dust (of the grave) of Aḥmad,*[3] *should not care even if he does not smell any other perfume in his lifetime.*[72] She has said in defence of the divine leadership of the Infallible Imāms (AS): *Our obedience is the system for the people and our leadership is a refuge from division.*[73]

One must not be neglectful in reaching out to the less deserving of her Shīᶜites, because her heart is connected to the hearts which are grieved for her grief and are pleased for her pleasure.

The Sayyids who are learned must reply to her greeting through spreading wisdom, good admonishment, and useful discussions with the orphans of Muhammad's Progeny. They must not let these pigeons with broken wings be deceived by the doubts of the opponents in the period of Occultation (of the Twelfth Imām (AS)). You must not allow the satans from the jinn and the men to hunt them down.

The Sayyids who are wealthy must reply to her greeting by not wasting their money in suppressing the basis of the constitution for which she gave her life; rather, they should spend in reviving the signs on the day of her martyrdom.

---

[2] Sayyid is a title given to a descendant of the Holy Prophet (SA); hence, the descendant of his daughter, Fāṭima (AS).

[3] Aḥmad is the name of the Messenger of Allāh, Muhammad (SA) given to him by his mother, Āmina (AS).

The common Sayyids should take notice of her heartbreaking words, which she said in her will to the Commander of the Faithful (AS): Give me *Ḥunūṭ* yourself, wash my body and shroud me during the night. Pray upon my body and bury me during the night. Do not inform anyone of my death.

The least response which has to be made is that to constitute for the isolation of her funeral (which can never be constituted), is to, in grief, hold banners on the eve of her martyrdom in every city and town. Also, wear clothing to mark the sorrow and march the streets saying to your great-grandmother: We will never forget you, or the hardships you bore. Whatever we may forget, but we will not forget your broken heart, afflicted body and your lost grave *till Allāh should give judgment, and He is the Best of the Judges.*[74]

O Allāh, for the sake of Fāṭima, her father, her husband, her sons, and for the sake of the mystery that is placed in her. Bless Fāṭima, her father, her husband and her sons, the count which is in Thy knowledge, an endless blessing, so long as Thy sovereign and reign continue. O Allāh, hasten the reappearance of Your guardian. O Allāh, put right all corruption from the affairs of the Muslims. O Allāh, forgive us and our brothers who have preceded us in faith. And our last cry is that all praise be to Allāh, Lord of the Worlds.

****

It has been reported that Abu ᶜAbd Allāh al-Sadiq (AS) said: "*Indeed, We have revealed it in the Night of Destiny [Laylat al-Qadr].*[75] The Night is Fāṭima."

This is the content of the tradition. The argument in each sentence requires explanation in detail. In continuation of the tradition that 'the Night is Fāṭima' he (AS) added: *Therefore, whoever recognises Fāṭima in her true recognition has comprehended the Night of Destiny.* She is the Night of Destiny, which no one can appreciate. The continuation of this sentence is: *Indeed, she was named Fāṭima because no creation is capable of recognising her.*[76]

Who is she? She is higher than being recognised by the creation! We must reflect upon this concept. This is a concept upon which the greatest of the human beings, i.e. uncorrupted intellectuals who have reached the zenith of integrity, must ponder to resolve. She is the Night of Destiny and the household of the Qur'an.

In another place in the Qur'ān it is stated: *Indeed, We have revealed it in a Blessed Night.*[77] In the explanation of this verse it has again appeared that the Blessed Night is Fāṭima. Therein, all wise affairs are made distinct.[78]

The following reasons are stated in the tradition regarding her name: *Indeed she was named Fāṭima because no creation is capable of recognising her.* The meaning of the word 'creation' is broader than the meaning of 'people'. The extent of this word includes the jinn and the humans. Moreover, the degree reaches the angels: *Thou (O Allāh) made angels reside in Thy skies and placed them high above from Thy earth. They have the most knowledge about Thee and Thy whole creation.*[79] Even they are incapable of this recognition.

What is the matter then? And who is this lady? What reality is concealed in her that she is above and superior to that which the intellects and imaginations may reach! For accomplishment of this issue one is in need of sound understanding, education with proof and reasoning, support from the most reliable proof, i.e. the Qur'ān and help from the most authentic traditions, because the creation is incapable of recognising her. But why, what is concealed in her that the creation is incapable of recognising her?

****

The following tradition has also appeared in both Shīᶜah and Sunnī sources, with little difference in its text. These are the words: "The Prophet (SA) came out and was holding the arm of Fāṭima (AS) and said: *Whoever has recognised her has recognised her...*" Pay attention to the words! Our gathering at this moment is a gathering which only needs a signal. What does it mean that he (SA) came out holding the arm of Fāṭima (AS)? This action with this lady holds the same position as the action to that man (ᶜAlī) on the Day of *Ghadīr*. He (SA) did this with the most exceptional man of the universe on the Day of *Ghadīr*. He held his arm and introduced him. Today he is holding the arm of this most exceptional lady of the universe and is saying: *Whoever has recognised her has recognised her; however, whosoever does not know her recognise her now.*

How did he introduce her? Step by step. The words of the Prophet (SA) contain their own manifestations for everyone. At first he (SA) said: *She is a part of me.* Do heed the word "part". This was the first step, and then from simplification he continued in detail. In the second step, he (SA) said: *She is my heart, which is between my two sides.*[80] When the Prophet (SA) says "I", it refers to other than 'my body'. Grammatically, 'body' is in the construct state and 'my' is a noun of a genitive construction.

Take notice of these expressions: 'my part' (not part of my body), 'my heart between my two sides'. These two sides are the sides of his body. She alone is a part of me. A part of me is other than a part of my body, and my heart between my two sides is other than a heart between the two sides of my body. This is from the essence of someone who is the beginning and origin of all human merits: *I was a Prophet when Adam was being created from water and earth.*[81] She is the heart of someone with such calibre. The implication of this is: if Fāṭima is taken from me, then I will remain but a body without life.

What has this lady become that she has attained such a status? She has become the heart of the two sides of knowledge and practice. The right side of the Prophet (SA) is knowledge and the left side is practice; the knowledge, which contains all the knowledge of all prophets (AS), the practice where the practices of all beloved ones have vanished. The heart which is found between these two sides of knowledge and practice is the Greatest Truthful Lady Fāṭima al-Zahrā'. Now it becomes clear why Allāh had said: They are Fāṭima, her father, her husband and her two sons.[82]

What have you done that you have become the centre? What have you done that you have become the pivot? What have you done that you have become the heart of the heart of this universe? What have you done to reach the status where the Seal of the Prophets (SA) says about you: *Whoever sends blessings on you will be with me wherever I am in Paradise.*[83]

What have you done? No one knows what you have done except for Allāh and the ones who are aware of the secrets of the treasures of Allāh. You are the one about whom the sixth Imām (AS) has said: *No creation is capable of recognising her.* After paying attention to what we have said, which is only (the beginning of) the alphabet of the reality, the words of the Imām become clear.

It has reached a place where: 'O Allāh, I ask Thee for the sake of Fāṭima and her father.' Do reflect and take notice of this, work out the deep understanding of these words. 'O Allāh, for the sake of Fāṭima, her father, her husband and her sons.'[84] The question is for the sake of Fāṭima, for the sake of Fāṭima's father, Fāṭima's husband and her sons.

The last step is the seal of the words. The Prophet (SA) was taken to the tree in the Paradise called *Ṭūbā* (blessedness). A fruit was picked from this tree. The sperm of Fāṭima was conceived. The spirit was blown into this drop.[85] God placed the most precious gem from His treasure in this spirit. Here lies the issue: 'O Allāh, I ask Thee for the sake of Fāṭima, her father, her husband, her sons and for the sake of the mystery that is placed in her.'[86] What is this mystery? The Night of Ascension, the Tree of *Ṭūbā* and the Fruit of the Paradise, were all preliminaries of this mystery. The explanation of this mystery requires another lecture.

****

O Daughter of the Prophet! Who are you? What status have you reached that whoever befriends you and dies, his grave becomes the visiting place of angels of mercy?[87] Then imagine, what must your grave be? The angels of mercy are like moths and the grave of the one that dies befriending you is like the candle. What must your own grave be like? Who goes around the place where you are buried? O Fakhr Rāzī! O Zamakhsharī! Have you understood what you have said? Did you understand what you wrote? Did you understand what is the mercy of Allāh? The mercy for which He says: *it encompasses everything.*[88]

He who disassociates with Fāṭima (AS) reaches a stage where he goes out of being a Shīᶜah and it is written on his forehead that he is disconnected from Allāh's mercy.[89] O Fakhr Rāzī, have you understood what you said? You have said, 'faith in existence and non-existence and in completion and incompletion is based upon the love of Fāṭima al-Zahrā' (AS). You have said this, but do you know where this statement ends? You have written, confirmed, and approved that the Prophet (SA) has said: *Hurting Fāṭima is hurting me. Fāṭima's anger is my anger.*[90]

I would like to talk for only a few moments regarding this sentence. The tradition which Fakhr has mentioned in his Commentary of Qur'ān has unhesitatingly declared that 'the Prophet (SA) said' and did not reject its report. The secret behind it is that this tradition is of a few types: some traditions say:

Fāṭima's pleasure is my pleasure and her anger is my anger.[91] Others say: *Indeed, Allāh is angered for your anger and He is pleased with your pleasure.*[92] As far as the chain of narration is concerned, not only has no researcher hesitated in accepting it, but also the leader and head of all critics, Shams al-Dīn al-Dhahabī, has also approved it.[93]

Have they understood what they have said? The implication of the word is that Fāṭima (AS) has the status of infallibility. However, it is not like the infallibility of Yacqūb (AS) or Yūsuf (AS), neither Mūsā, (AS) nor cIsā (AS). Nor is it like the infallibility of Ibrāhīm (AS). Fāṭima (AS) has reached the status of the infallibility of the Seal of the Messengers (SA). *Indeed, Allāh is angered for your anger and is pleased with your pleasure.*[94]

The question from Fakhr al-Dīn al-Rāzī is if Fāṭima is not infallible from mistakes and personal desires, then forcibly her pleasure and anger, and, if the slightest deviation from righteousness is found in her action, then the pleasure and anger of Allāh would be related to voidance. Thus, based upon evidence, Fāṭima (AS) has reached a horizon and has taken an abode which no imagination can comprehend. It is not the time for me to explain that it is not infallibility; rather, it has reached beyond infallibility. Pay good attention!

What is infallibility? Infallibility is when the pleasure and anger of a human being surpasses animal nature. It reaches the limits of wisdom. It should even cross human nature and reach divinity. If one's pleasure is the pleasure of God and anger is the anger of God, then this human being reaches a level where he becomes angry when God becomes angry. Whenever God becomes pleased, he becomes pleased.

However, the issue is above this. We say that Fāṭima has reached a stage where whenever God is angered, she is angered and whenever God is pleased, she is pleased. However, what the

Prophet (SA) has said is: *God is angered for her anger and is pleased for her pleasure.* This is where the intellect becomes deficient.

****

The experts on Qur'ān and Hadīth have unanimously accepted what we want to say today and the summary of that is this: The Prophet (SA) and the Christians from Najrān came out to curse one another [*mubāhalah*]. He was wearing a black cloak on that promised day. That is after establishing the proof: *Indeed the likeness of Jesus [ᶜIsā] is with Allāh as the likeness of Adam.*[95] After this decisive scientific proof was established, the position came to dispute. The concepts are clear before you all. What is significant is what the Sunnīs have transmitted. The following should be addressed.

It came to a stage of cursing one another [*mubāhalah*]. What is the reality of cursing one another? This can be established from the words of the Christian Archbishop; specifically, that when he came out he was wearing a black cloak. What was his situation when he came out? Whatever is being said is from the finest sources of commentaries on Qur'ān and books of traditions. They do not have any connection with the Shīᶜah school of thought.

He came out while he was holding Ḥusayn (AS) in his arm. The Master of the Martyrs [Sayyid al-Shuhadā'] was old enough to walk, but the state in which the Prophet (SA) came out was that he was holding Ḥusayn (AS) in his arm. This was the way he made his appearance. With his other hand he was holding the hand of Ḥasan (AS). Pay good attention at the detail in the narration. He was walking in front. Behind him was Fāṭima al-Zahrā' (AS) and behind her was ᶜAlī ibn Abū Ṭālib (AS). This was the state in which he came out.

This is the Prophet (SA) for whom the Qur'ān says: *He does not speak out of desire.*[96] This in itself is another topic. Someone who does not speak out of desire does not do anything out of desire either. He is the one that: *Whatever the Messenger gives you, accept it, and from whatever he forbids you, keep back.*[97] It is he whose *sunnah* is not only his words, but also his approvals and actions. His motion is *sunnah*, and his motionlessness is *sunnah*. All of his states and conditions are connected to the status of: *Then he drew near, then he bowed, so he was the measure of two bows or closer still.*[98] He is the conclusion of the world. This is the Seal of the Prophets (SA). He is the essence of existence and is the first person in the existing world.

Every look is a world of wisdom of such a human being. His every action is the fountain of the oceans of all arts. When he is in front, ᶜAlī (AS) at the back, and Fāṭima (AS) in the middle, then this in itself has an implication. The implication of this action is that Fāṭima (AS) is the barrier between the highest level of prophethood and the greatest level of guardianship. The implication of this action is that Fāṭima's position is pivotal and central between the best revelation, its deliverance, and explanation of the revelation. In front of Fāṭima (AS) is the deliverance of revelation and behind her is the explanation of the revelation. This is Fāṭima al-Zahrā'. Her status is unknown to all of the worlds.

This is the state in which he (SA) came out. What was the state? What were the issues? The Christian Archbishop, the head of all bishops, announced to all the Najrān: "I see faces coming to us that if such faces willed they would move the mountains from their positions. All of this valley would burn with fire. If they open their lips for prayer and lift their hands to the heavens, then no Christian would remain on the surface of the earth."

I wish the understanding of this Christian bishop tallied with the transmission of Fakhr Rāzī! However, the misfortune is that the narration is from Fakhr Rāzī, but the cognisance is from the Christian bishop. This is in itself a great problem. Then the Christian bishop said, "They should not lift their hands in prayer at any cost." When the Prophet (SA) had come out, he turned around, looked at these people and said: *When I pray then say Amen.*[99]

Take notice of the words, "when I pray then say 'Amen.'" What is the meaning of this statement? O Fakhr Rāzī! O Zamakhsharī! O Bayḍāwī! The meaning of this statement is this: 'my action is a reflection of the revelation and the revelation is: *But whoever disputes with you in this matter after what has come to you of knowledge, then say: Come let us call our sons and your sons and our women and your women and our near people and your near people, then let us be earnest in prayer.*[100] All must gather and then let us be earnest in prayer. The meaning of this statement is that, being the Seal of the Prophets, my prayer is required. However, the condition for the actualisation of this requirement is Fāṭima al-Zahrā. Therefore, her amen must be added to my prayer.'

Such is the revelation and such is the practice of the Prophet (SA) that the prayer of Zahrā (AS) is a condition. It is impossible for the requirement to have an effect without the condition. Thus, it is not logical to pray at such a time, in dispute with the Christians of Najrān. Therefore, when the hands of the Prophet (SA) go up (in prayer), then there must be four sets of hands rising up to the heavens at the same time. If this is how it is, then who is ᶜAlī (AS)? Who is Fāṭima (AS)? Who is Ḥasan (AS)? Who is Ḥusayn (AS)?

****

From Ibn Qutaybah to Muhammad Farīd Wajdī, all have written in the encyclopaedia that ('Umar) came to the house of al-Zahrā (AS) and said, "O ᶜAlī, come out for paying allegiance, or I will burn down this house with its household." Who were the dwellers of this house? O Fakhr Rāzī! O Qādī Bayḍāwī! O Zamakhsharī! O Jalāl al-Dīn al-Siyūṭī! You are a man of understanding, why did you not understand? Such a person came and said: 'O ᶜAlī, come out for paying allegiance, or I will burn down this house with its dwellers.' *And say: Then Allāh's is the conclusive argument.*[101]

Someone said to him: 'There is Fāṭima (AS) in this house.' There is depth in this statement that there is Fāṭima (AS) in this house. The implication of this statement is that in this house is the person for whom the Prophet (SA) said: *Hurting her is hurting me and hurting me is hurting God.* From Ibn Qutaybah to Farīd Wajdī, all have written that that person said: 'And even if!'

I have a question. Please pay good attention! By God, even if one weeps blood on this tragedy it is little. What kind of allegiance is this, for he said: 'O ᶜAlī come out or I will burn down this house with its household.' It is the same allegiance for which this person came to this house and said what he said. The same person later said, "The allegiance to Abū Bakr was an error, Allāh protected the people [*ummah*] from its evil."[102]

By God, the evidence is clear for the entire world. This man has said it himself and this is in Ṣaḥīḥ al-Bukhārī. The one who came to burn down the house with ᶜAlī, Fāṭima, Ḥasan and Ḥusayn (AS) in it, Bukhārī has written in his Ṣaḥīḥ that he said: 'The allegiance to Abū Bakr was an error, Allāh protected the people from this evil.'

O man! If the allegiance was such an allegiance, according to your own confession, O Sunnī scholar! The man who has said this, is he sane or insane? If he is insane, then there is nothing to argue. However, if he is sane, then the confession of the sane against themselves is permitted (and a proof against them). The allegiance was an error according to this man. He came to burn

Fāṭima (AS) in order to guard this allegiance. Is there anyone more oppressed in this world than this holy lady? By God, the tragedy is greater than whatever we can imagine!

****

She was a mystery! She herself was a mystery! The greatest mystery of Allāh! Her heart was a mystery! Whatever was in her heart was a mystery! Her pains were a mystery! Her tragedy was a mystery! Whatever she went through was a mystery! Her position is a mystery! Her status is a mystery! A mystery within a mystery! The grave that hides her body is a mystery!

What have you done and to where have you reached? What I can say is that she did something through which she gave life to everyone from Adam to Muhammad (AS). Through her action the name of God was given life. She did something through which all the honours of Allāh were given life.

If a believer dies, the first gift he is presented with in his grave is that it is said to him: *All those who attended your funeral are forgiven.* She knew this. Therefore, she said: *O ᶜAlī, do not inform anyone of it (my death).*[103] This is what caused the tumult. The world must contemplate upon this and discover what happened. When the Prophet (SA) parted from this world, Fāṭima (AS) was absolutely active and healthy. However, after 75 days, the night in which her body was prepared for ritual bathing, I cannot say what it was. The expression used is that *she was like a shadow.*[104] The meaning is that when her body was placed for bathing, it was (so slim) like a shadow.

There did not remain but a soul that feared,
Or a slight pale of her human (form)!

****

This is Fāṭima al-Zahrā' (AS). This is the human ḥūrī. This is the Greatest Truthful Lady. She is a human being which is the pivot in the circle of the highest level of prophethood and the greatest level of guardianship. By God, the status of al-Zahrā' is unknown to the world and to the human beings. The status of Fāṭima (AS) is unknown in the Sunnī institutions, but that is not so regretful. However, in the country of Fāṭima! This is a country of al-Zahrā'. This is a country of Fāṭima (AS). In the country of Fāṭima al-Zahrā' (AS), for the non-Islamic festival Nawrūz, there is an official holiday. Yet, there is not one holiday in this country for the martyrdom of Fāṭima al-Zahrā' (AS). Her status is unknown! Her status is unknown!

When her status becomes known, only then will it become apparent that the Proof of God (AS) said: When she lifts her head from the grave, God will send two groups each of seventy thousand angels to receive her. Seventy thousand angels holding the banner of *Takbīr*, and seventy thousand holding the banner of *Tasbīḥ*. They will come to welcome Fāṭima (AS). After she settles down in her place... For Ibrāhīm (AS) such a regard has not come. God has not poured out such a regard from His treasure for Mūsā ibn 'Imrān (AS). Nor did He give such a regard for ᶜIsā bin Maryam (AS). God will open an endless regard for Fāṭima (AS).

Jibra'īl (AS) will come and say to her: Ask your wish, it will be granted. Your wish has no limit. Whatever you wish, ask for it. It does not have a limit. What is her wish from God? You are all people of exactness. Do reflect upon this, realise how high this concept is. What is her wish from God? O scholars, this is what is significant: a wish is always a reward. Reward is other than deed. Deed and reward are different from each other.

However this is Fāṭima (AS) to whom it is said, Ask your wish, it will be granted. She will say: *O Lord, show me al-Ḥasan and al-Ḥusayn (AS).* She will want the deed. When she will wish for the deed, it will come to an end. What does that mean? It means, O God! Show me exactly whatever they have done (against my sons). This will be shown to her. Al-Ḥusayn's jugular vein will have blood flowing out.[105]

****

The Prophet (SA) entered before Fāṭima (AS). When he came in, he saw that she was wearing a cloak made from camelhair. The dress was such a dress! What was the purpose? She was grinding the hand-mill. It came into his sight and he saw that she had not slept all night due to staying up in worship. When she got up in the morning, this was her dress. This was her job! This was heartbreaking for the Prophet (SA). This is not insignificant. When her eyes shed tears, then the heart starts crying. The Messenger of Allāh (SA) started to cry and said to his daughter: *Be patient at the bitterness of this world!*[106]

While Siyūṭī, Ibn Dallāl, Ibn Najjār and the rest have narrated what had happened, we (I) do not understand. What we do understand is that the Prophet (SA) moved on and left. Jibr'īl came down to him and brought this verse: *And soon will your Lord give you so that you shall be well pleased.*[107]

The unique man of the world, who did not fold his knees at the battle of Khaybar, whose back was not broken in the battle of Khandaq, passed the night of migration smoothly. However, he was distraught in the night in which Fāṭima (AS) passed away. ᶜAlī (AS) said: *O Messenger of Allāh, my patience about your chosen (daughter) has been exhausted.*[108] He did not share this pain with anyone. Who did he have to share this with? There was no one who could understand what pain he was going through, except he who was addressed and said that O Messenger of Allāh, my patience about your chosen one has been exhausted.

****

She is not someone who can be recognised. Only ᶜAlī (AS) recognised her and said: *As to my grief, it knows no bounds, and as to my nights, they will remain sleepless.*[109] He had recognised her and had placed both this world and the hereafter under his feet. However, the grief of Fāṭima's death crushed him, only because he knew who she was.

****

What happened that she was buried during the night? Why was it that this had to happen? What happened? This is not an incident which a Muslim can ignore, unless there is flaw in his belief. Is it possible for someone to believe in the Prophet (SA) and ignore the burial by night of Fāṭima al-Zahrā, the Greatest Truthful Lady, the Great Honour of the Almighty, and the Centre of the Five Holy Ones? How can one hide such a crime? It is a crime which should be the focus of argument of all of our learned and common people. What happened and how did things reach such a stage?

O God, forgive us so that we do not share the oppression upon Fāṭima (AS)! O God, forgive us so that we are not held responsible for that weeping, for those tears and cries.

****

O Allāh, for the sake of Fāṭima, her father, her husband, her sons, and for the sake of the mystery that is placed in her. Bless and send peace upon Fāṭima, her father, her husband and her sons, the count which is in Thy knowledge, an endless blessing, so long as Thy Sovereign and Clemency continue. O Allāh, curse her enemies and the ones who have usurped her rights, the count which is in Thy knowledge, an endless and eternal curse, so long as Thy Subdual and Justice continue. And the last of our cry is that all Praise be to Allāh, Lord of the Worlds.

---

1 *Biḥār al-Anwār*: vol. 66, pp 293.
2 Qur'ān: 24: 35.
3 Ibid: 14: 1.
4 Ibid: 23: 14.
5 Ibid: 7: 180.
6 Ibid: 30: 30.
7 Ibid: 5: 3.
8 *ᶜUyūn Akhbār al-Riḍā* (AS): vol. 2, pp 66, ch. 31, *ḥadīth* no. 298, & *Al-Tawḥīd*: pp 307, & *Al-Mustadrak ᶜalā al-Ṣaḥīḥayn*: vol. 3, pp 126, & *Majmᶜ al-Zawā'id*: vol. 9, pp 111, and other Sunnī sources.
9 Qur'ān: 14: 24-5.
10 *Al-Amālī* by Shaykh Ṣadūq: pp 78, ch. 7, *ḥadīth* no. 3, & *Musnad* by Aḥmad bin Ḥanbal: vol. 3, pp 37.
11 Qur'ān: 9: 33.
12 Ibid: 39: 69.
13 Ibid: 53: 3.
14 *Ṣaḥīḥ al-Bukhārī*: vol. 4, pp 210, ch. Merits of the Prophets' Relatives, & with little difference in *Al-Iydāh*: pp 541 and other Shīᶜah and Sunnī sources.
15 *Ṣaḥīḥ al-Bukhārī*: vol. 4, pp 210, ch. Merits of the Prophets' Relatives, & with little difference in *Al-Ṭarā'f*: pp 262 and other Shīᶜah and Sunnī sources.
16 *Al-Kāfī*: vol. 1, pp 442, *ḥadīth* no. 10.
17 *Al-Amālī* by Shaykh Ṭūsī: pp 78, & *Al-Mustadrak ᶜalā al-Ṣaḥīḥayn*: vol. 3, pp 154.
18 Enlightenments of John: ch. 12.
19 Qur'ān: 44: 4.
20 Ibid: 3: 61.
21 Ibid: 55: 19, & *Al-Khiṣāl*: pp 165.
22 Ibid: 76: 9, & *Al-Irshād*: vol. 1, pp 178.
23 *Tārīkh Baghdād*: vol. 1, pp 274.
24 *Al-Mustadrak ᶜalā al-Ṣaḥīḥayn*: vol. 3, pp 153.
25 Qur'ān: 57: 12.
26 Ibid: 54: 55.
27 *Mīzān al-Iᶜtidāl*: vol. 2, pp 131.

[28] *Tafsīr Furāt al-Kūfī*: pp 446.
[29] Qur'ān: 3: 164.
[30] Ibid: 108.
[31] *Wasā'il al-Shī'ah*: vol. 11, pp 200.
[32] *Al-Amālī* by Shaykh Ṣadūq: pp 688, & *Al-Khiṣāl*: pp 414, & *ʿIlal al-Sharā'iʿ*: vol. 1, pp 178.
[33] *Tafsīr Furāt al-Kūfī*: pp 581, *ḥadīth* no. 747.
[34] *Maʿānī al-Akhbār*: pp 64.
[35] *Manāqib Āl-Abū Ṭālib*: vol. 3, pp 111.
[36] *Al-Kharā'ij wa-al-Jarā'iḥ*: vol. 2, pp 529.
[37] *Manāqib Āl-Abū Ṭālib*: vol. 3, pp 117.
[38] *Manāqib Āl-Abū Ṭālib*: vol. 3, pp 117.
[39] Qur'ān: 21: 47.
[40] Ibid: 7: 8.
[41] Ibid: 58: 11.
[42] Ibid: 46: 19.
[43] Ibid: 56: 1-3.
[44] Ibid: 99: 6-8.
[45] Ibid: 76: 1-3.
[46] Ibid: 45: 13.
[47] Ibid: 14: 34.
[48] Ibid: 35: 28.
[49] Ibid: 2: 255.
[50] *Al-Amālī* By Shaykh Mufīd: pp 130, & with little difference in *Al-Mustadrak ʿalā al-Ṣaḥīḥayn*: vol. 3, pp 153.
[51] *Al-Kāfī*: vol. 1, pp 459.
[52] *Man Lā Yaḥḍuruhu al-Faqīh*: vol. 2, pp 595.
[53] *Biḥār al-Anwār*: vol. 45, pp 53.
[54] *Biḥār al-Anwār*: vol. 43, pp 177.
[55] *Biḥār al-Anwār*: vol. 79, pp 106.
[56] *Daʿā'im al-Islām*: vol. 1, pp 232.
[57] *Nahjul Balāghah*: sermon no. 202.
[58] *Al-Kāfī*: vol. 1, pp 459.
[59] Ibid.
[60] Qur'ān: 42: 23.
[61] *Kanz al-Fawā'id*: pp 154.
[62] Qur'ān: 5: 35.
[63] Ibid: 3: 19.

[64] *Kitāb al-Tawḥīd*: pp 152.
[65] Qur'ān: 5: 54.
[66] *Biḥār al-Anwār*: vol. 43, pp 214.
[67] Qur'ān: 3: 18.
[68] Ibid: 13: 43.
[69] Ibid: 36: 58.
[70] Ibid: 59: 23.
[71] *Biḥār al-Anwār*: vol. 43, pp 175.
[72] *Manāqib Āl-Abū Ṭālib*: vol. 1, pp 208.
[73] *Al-Iḥtijāj*: vol. 1, pp 134.
[74] Qur'ān: 10: 109.
[75] Qur'ān: 97: 1.
[76] *Biḥār al-Anwār*: vol. 43, pp 65, ch. 3, *ḥadīth* no. 58, & *Tafsīr Furāt al-Kūfī*: pp 581, *ḥadīth* no. 747.
[77] Qur'ān: 44: 3.
[78] Aḥmad ibn Mihrān and ᶜAlī ibn Ibrāhīm both reported on the authority of Muḥammad ibn ᶜAlī, on the authority of al-Ḥasan ibn Rāshid, on the authority of Yaᶜqūb ibn Jaᶜfar ibn Ibrāhīm saying: I was in the presence of Abū al-Ḥasan Mūsā (AS), when a Christian came to him and asked him some questions. One of the questions was: "Tell me about *Ḥā Mīm. By the manifesting Book, verily We revealed it on a blessed night; We have ever been warning therein, all wise affairs are made distinct.* What is the hidden explanation?" He (AS) explained, "As for *Ḥā Mīm*, then that is Muḥammad (SA) in the Book revealed upon Hūd (AS), and it is reduced in letters. As for the Manifesting Book, then that is the Commander of the Faithful (ᶜAlī ibn Abū Ṭālib (AS)). And as for the Night, then that is Fāṭima (AS). Furthermore, the verse, 'therein all wise affairs are made distinct' refers to the birth of wise men from her." Al-Kāfī: vol. 1 pp 479, ch. Birth of Abū al-Ḥasan Mūsā ibn Jaᶜfar, *ḥadīth* no. 4, *Biḥār al-Anwār*: vol. 24, pp 319, ch. 67, *ḥadīth* 28 & vol. 48, pp 87, ch. 4, *ḥadīth* 28. *Ta'wīl al-Āyāt al-Dhāhirah*: pp 555.
[79] *Nahjul Balaghah*: sermon no. 109 from Imām ᶜAlī ibn Abū Ṭālib (AS).
[80] It is reported on the authority of Mujāhid that he said: The Prophet (SA) came out of his house and he was holding the arm of Fāṭima (AS) and said, "Whoever has recognised her has recognised her; however, whosoever does not know her, know her now. She is Fāṭima daughter of Muḥammad (SA). She is a part of me. She is my heart and soul that is between my two sides. Therefore, whoever hurts her has hurt me and whoever hurts me has hurt Allāh." *Biḥār al-*

Anwār: vol. 43, pp 54, ch. 3, & pp 80, ch. 3 & *Kashf al-Ghummah*: vol. 1, pp 466-7.

[81] Even though the angels prostrated once to Adam (AS), it was due to Muḥammad (SA). Up to the Day of Judgement, all angels and human beings will do so every moment. While Adam (AS) was the direction of prayer [*qiblah*] of the angels, Allāh made Muḥammad (SA) the leader of prayer for all the prophets on the Night of Ascension. Therefore, he (SA) became the leader of Adam as well. If Adam (AS) was created from earth then Muḥammad (SA) was created from light. He (SA) said, "I was a Prophet when Adam was being created from water and earth." If Adam (AS) was the first creation, then Muḥammad (SA) was before him. *Biḥār al-Anwār*: vol. 16, pp 402, ch. 12, *ḥadīth* no. 1, & vol. 18, pp 278, ch. 2, *ḥadīth* no. 1, & *Al-Anwār*: pp 2, & *'Awālī al-Liālī*: vol. 4, pp 121, *ḥadīth* no. 200, & *Miftāh al-Falāh*: pp 41, & Al-Manāqib: vol. 1, pp 214.

[82] *Mafātīh al-Jinān*: *ḥadīth al-Kisā'*.

[83] It is reported on the authority of the Commander of the Faithful (AS) from Fāṭima (AS) that she said: The Messenger of Allāh (SA) said to me, "O Fāṭima, whoever sends blessings on you, Allāh will forgive him and will join him with me wherever I am in the Paradise." *Biḥār al-Anwār*: vol. 97, pp 194, ch. 5, *ḥadīth* no. 10, & vol. 43, pp 55, ch. 3, & *Mustadrak al-Wasā'il*: vol. 10, pp 211, ch. 14, *ḥadīth* no. 2-11877, & *Kashf al-Ghummah*: vol. 1, pp 472.

[84] Some recent Sunnī scholars have said in the book: *Khulāṣat al-Kalām fī Umrā al-Balad al-Ḥarām*, and some Gnostics have a supplication containing the words: 'O Allāh, the Lord of Kaᶜbah and its Founder, (by) Fāṭima, her father, her husband and her sons, give light to my eyes, vision, heart and soul.' The supplication has been tried for restoring vision. Allāh will enlighten the sight of whoever recites it while applying kohl to the eyes. *Mustadrak al-Wasā'il*: vol. 1, pp 446, ch. 78, *ḥadīth* no. 9-1123.

[85] On the authority of Ṣadūq it has been reported, on the authority of Aḥmad ibn ᶜAlī ibn Ibrāhīm, on the authority of his father, on the authority of his grandfather, on the authority of ᶜAlī ibn Maᶜbad, on the authority of Aḥmad ibn ᶜUmar, on the authority of Zayd al-Naqāb, on the authority of Abān ibn Taghlab saying that Abū ᶜAbd Allāh (AS) said, "The Prophet (SA) used to kiss (his daughter) Fāṭima (AS) very frequently. Therefore, (his wife) 'Āyisha rebuked him for that and said, 'O Messenger of Allāh, why do you frequently kiss Fāṭima?' He (SA) replied to her, 'Indeed, when I ascended to the heavens, Jibr'īl took me to the tree of *Tūbā* and gave me a date from it. So I ate it. That became a part of my body. When I came back to the earth, I conceived Fāṭima in the

womb of Khadījah. Hence, whenever I kiss her I smell the heavenly tree *Ṭūbā* in her.''" *Biḥār al-Anwār*: vol. 18, pp 315, ch. 3, *ḥadīth* no. 27, & vol. 8, pp 120, ch. 23, *ḥadīth* no. 10, & vol. 18, pp 364, ch. 3, *ḥadīth* no. 68, & vol. 43, pp 6, ch. 1, *ḥadīth* no. 6, & *A'lām al-Wara'*: pp 150, & *Ta'wīl al-Āyāt al-Ẓāhirah*: pp 240, ch. 13, & *Tafsīr al-ᶜAyyāshī*: vol. 2, pp 212, ch. 13, *ḥadīth* no. 46, & *Tafsīr al-Qummī*: vol. 1, pp 365.

86 Refer to footnote no. 10.

87 The Writer of Al-Kashshāf has reported on the authority of the Prophet (SA) that he said: "Beware, whoever dies in the love of the Household of Muḥammad (SA) dies the death of a martyr. Beware, whoever dies in the love of the Household of Muḥammad, dies the death of one who has been forgiven. Beware, he who dies in the love of the Household of Muḥammad, dies the death of one who has repented. Beware, he who dies in the love of the Household of Muḥammad, dies the death of a believer of complete faith. Beware he who dies in the love of the Household of Muḥammad, the angel of death first gives him the good news of Paradise, and then the (two angels) *Munkir* and *Nakīr*. Beware, he who dies in the love of the Household of Muḥammad, is taken to Paradise like a bride is taken to the house of her husband. Beware, whosoever dies in the love of the Household of Muḥammad (SA), two doors are opened up in his grave which lead to Paradise. Beware, whoever dies in the love of the Household of Muḥammad (SA), Allāh makes his grave the visiting place of the angels of mercy. Beware, whoever dies in the love of the Household of Muḥammad (SA), dies on the *sunnah* and *jamāᶜat*. Beware, whoever dies in the hatred of the Household of Muḥammad (SA), will come on the Day of Judgment in a state where it will be written on his forehead: 'he is hopeless from Allāh's mercy. Beware, whosoever dies in the hatred of the Household of Muḥammad (SA), will die the death of a disbeliever. Beware, he who dies in the hatred of the Household of Muḥammad (SA), will not smell the sweet smell of the Paradise. *Biḥār al-Anwār*: vol. 23, pp 233, ch. 13, & vol. 65, pp 137, ch. 18, *ḥadīth* no. 76, & *Bashārat al-Muṣṭafā*: pp 197, & *Jāmiᶜ al-Akhbār*: pp 165, ch. 131, & *Saᶜd al-Suᶜūd*: pp 141, & *Al-Ṭarā'if*: vol. 1, pp 159, *ḥadīth* no. 248, & *Al-ᶜUmdah*: pp 54, ch. 9, *ḥadīth* no. 52, & *Kashf al-Ghummah*: vol. 1, pp 107.

88 *And ordain for us good in this world's life and m the hereafter, for surely we turn to Thee. He said: (As for) My chastisement, I will afflict with it whom I please, and My mercy encompasses all things; so I will ordain it (especially) for those who guard (against evil) and pay the poor-rate, and those who believe in Our communications.* Qur'ān: 7: 156.

[89] Refer to footnote no. 13.

[90] *Tafsīr al-Rāzī*: vol. 9, pp 160, & vol. 27, pp 166, & vol. 32, pp 141.

[91] On the authority of Zādān, on the authority of Salmān al-Fārisī (RA), who eliminated the source of report, said: "O Salmān, whoever loves my daughter Fāṭima will be with me in the Paradise and whoever hates her will be in the Hellfire. O Salmān, Fāṭima's love is useful in one hundred places, the easiest of those places are: death, grave, weighing (of deeds), *Ṣirāṭ* (the bridge over the hellfire) and accountability. Thus, whoever my daughter Fāṭima is pleased with, I am pleased with and whoever I am pleased with, Allāh is pleased with him. Whoever my daughter Fāṭima is displeased with, I am displeased with and whoever I am displeased with, Allāh is displeased with. O Salmān, woe be to the one who oppresses her, oppresses her spouse ᶜAlī (AS), her progeny and her followers. *Yanābīᶜ al-Mawaddah Li-Dhawil Qurbā*: vol. 2, pp 332, *ḥadīth* no. 970.

[92] *Al-Mustadrak* by Al-Ḥākim al-Naysābūrī: vol. 3, pp 153, & *Majmᶜ al-Zawā'id* by Al-Haythamī: vol. 9, pp 203, & *Al-Muᶜjam al-Kabīr* by Ṭibrānī: vol. 1, pp 108, *ḥadīth* no. 182, & vol. 22, pp 401, & *Naẓm Durar al-Simṭayn* by al-Zarandī al-Ḥanafī: pp 177, & *Kanz al-ᶜUmmāl* by Al-Muttaqī al-Hindī: vol. 12, pp 222, *ḥadīth* no. 34237, & vol. 13, pp 674, *ḥadīth* no. 37725, *Usd al-Ghābbah* by Ibn al-Athyr: vol. 5, pp 522, & *Tārīkh Baghdād* by Ibn al-Najjār al-Baghdādī: vol. 2, pp 140, & Mīzān al-Iᶜtidāl by Al-Dhahabī: vol. 1, pp 535, no. 2002, & vol. 2, pp 491, no. 4560, & *Al-Iṣābah* by Ibn Ḥajar: vol. 8, pp 265-6, & *Yanābīᶜ al-Mawaddah Li-Dhawil Qurbā* by Al-Qundūzī: vol. 2, pp 46, *ḥadīth* no. 293, & pp 56, *ḥadīth* no. 32, pp 58, *ḥadīth* no. 40, pp 72, *ḥadīth* no. 24, & *ᶜIlal al-Dār Quṭnī* by Al-Dār Quṭnī: vol. 3, pp 103, *ḥadīth* no. 305, & *Tahdhīb al-Kamāl* by Al-Mazī: vol. 3, pp 250, & *Subul al-Hudā wa-al-Rashād* by Al-Ṣāliḥī al-Shāmī: vol. 11, pp 44.

[93] Ibid.

[94] Ibid.

[95] Qur'ān: 3: 59.

[96] Ibid: 53: 3.

[97] Ibid: 59: 7.

[98] Ibid: 53: 8-9.

[99] The second issue: It is narrated that after he (SA) conveyed his proofs to the Christians of Najrān, and they continued with their ignorance, he said to them, "Indeed, Allāh has commanded me that if you do not accept my proof, then I will earnest in prayer with you." Therefore they said, "O Abū al-Qāsim, we will return to discuss our affair and come back to you." When they returned, they said to ᶜĀqib, who was a man of vision, "O servant of Christ, what is your

view?" He said, "O group of Christians, by God, you have come to know that Muḥammad is a Messenger of God. He has come to you with the truth about Jesus. By God, there is not a single group of people who have gone to earnest in prayer against a Prophet but their big and small have been destroyed. However, if you still go to earnest in prayer against him then it will be an uproot (of all Christians), but if you do not then your religion will continue. Leave the man and return to your land." The Messenger of Allāh (SA) came out wearing a cloak made of black hair. He was holding al-Ḥusayn (AS) in his arm and al-Ḥasan (AS) was holding his hand, while, Fāṭima (AS) was behind him and ᶜAlī (AS) was behind her. He was telling them, "When I pray then say amen." The Bishop of Najrān said, "O Christians, I am seeing faces that if they prayed to God to move the mountain from its place, He would. Do not earnest in prayer against them, otherwise you shall be destroyed and there will not remain a single Christian up to the Day of Judgment." Then they said, "O Abū al-Qāsim, we have come to a conclusion not to earnest in prayer against you. We have decided to leave you on your religion." He (SA) responded, "If you do not wish to earnest in prayer against me then submit to Islam. You will have all the rights that the Muslims have." They refused to do so. So he (AS) offered, "I will go to battle against you." They answered, "We do not have the strength to go to battle against the Arabs. However, we will make a peace that you do not to go to battle against us and do not reject us to follow our religion.

[100] Qur'ān: 3: 61.

[101] Ibid: 6: 149.

[102] *Ṣaḥīḥ al-Bukhārī*: vol. 8, pp 26, *Kitāb al-Muḥārabīn min ahlil kufr wa-al-radda: bāb rajm al-ḥublā*, & *Al-Fāyiq fī gharīb al-ḥadīth*: vol. 3, pp 50, & *Sharḥ Nahj al-Balāghah* by Ibn Abū al-Ḥadīd: vol. 2, 26, 29 and other places of this book, & *Al-Bidāyah wa-al-Nihāyah*: vol. 12, pp 338, & *Tārīkh al-Khulafā'*: pp 67, & *Gharīb al-Ḥadīth*: vol. 3, pp 355, & *Al-Nihāyah fī Gharīb al-ḥadīth*: vol. 3, pp 467, & *Al-Miᶜyār wa-al-Muwāzanah*: pp 38 and 231, & *Muṣannaf* by Ibn Abū Shaybah: vol. 7, pp 615 and 616, vol. 8, pp 570, & *Al-Tifāt by Ibn Habān*: vol. 2, pp 156, & *Tārīkh al-Yaᶜqūbī*: vol. 2, pp 158, & *Subul al-Hudā wa-al-Rashād*: vol. 11, pp 127, & *Musnad Aḥmad bin Ḥanbal*: vol. 1, pp 55, & *Al-Muṣannaf* by ᶜAbd al-Razzāq: vol 5, pp 442 and 445, & *Al-Sunan al-Kubrā* by Al-Nisā'ī: vol. 4, pp 272 and 273 and 433, & *Ṣaḥīḥ Ibn Habbān*: vol. 2, pp 148 and 155 and …, & *Tārīkh Madīnat Damishq*: vol. 30, pp 283, & *Tārīkh al-Tabarī*: vol. 2, pp 446, *Al-Sīrat al-Nabawiyyah* by Ibn Kathīr: vol. 4, pp 487, and other Sunnī books.

[103] *Biḥār al-Anwār*: vol. 43, pp 234, ch. 7.

[104] It was reported to us on the authority of Abū Ja^cfar (AS), on the authority of his father (AS) that the Prophet (SA) secretly told Fāṭima (AS) that she is going to be the first from his household to join him in the hereafter. When the Prophet (SA) parted from this world, the people harmed her so much so that she was bedridden. She grew thin, the flesh on her body dissolved, and she became like a shadow. She lived after the Prophet (SA) for seventy days. When the time of her death came close, she said to Asmā' bint ᶜUmays, "How will I be carried since I have become like a shadow, and my skin has dried up to my bones?"
Asmā' said to her, "O daughter of the Messenger of Allāh (SA), indeed the decree of Allāh is ordained for you. I will make something for you which I saw in Abyssinia [Ḥabashah]."
She (AS) asked, "What is it?"
Asmā' replied, "A coffin. They place it over the deceased on the deathbed, covering the body."
She (AS) said, "Do so." When she passed away, Asmā' made the coffin for her. It was the first coffin made for a woman in Islam." *Mustadrak al-Wasā'il*: vol. 2, pp 361, ch. 43, *ḥadīth* no. 5-2191, & *Biḥār al-Anwār*: vol. 78, pp 282, ch. 7, *ḥadīth* no. 40, & *Daᶜā'im al-Islām*: vol. 1, pp 232, *dhikr al-sīr bi-al-janā'iẓ*.
[105] On the authority of Sulaymān ibn Muḥammad, who has reported it from his chain of transmission, on the authority of Ibn ᶜAbbās saying: I heard the Commander of the Faithful saying, "One day the Messenger of Allāh (SA) entered the presence of Fāṭima (AS), while she was sorrowful. The Prophet (SA) asked her, 'O my daughter, what has made you sad?' She answered, 'I fell in remembrance of the Day of Resurrection and people standing disgracefully on the Day of Judgment.' Hence, he responded, 'It is a very difficult day, O my daughter. However, Jibra'īl has informed me from Allāh, the Mighty and High, that I will be the first one to part from the earth on the Day of Judgment. Then it will be my forefather Abraham (AS), then your spouse ᶜAlī ibn Abū Ṭālib (AS). Then Allāh will send down Jibra'īl with seventy thousand angels to you. He will place seven domes of light on your grave. After that (the angel) Isrāfīl will come to you with three clothings of light. Thus, he will stand near your head and call to you, "O Fāṭima, daughter of Muḥammad, get up for your resurrection." Hence, you will stand up peacefully, without fear and fully covered. Isrāfīl will give you the clothing and you will put them on. Rawfā'īl will bring for you a she-camel made of light, whose bridles will be of fresh pearls and it will have a sedan made of gold. You will ride it and Rawfā'īl will sit before you holding the bridles. In front of you will be seventy thousand angels holding

banners of 'Glory be to Allāh' in their hands. When you appear for the first time in your journey, seventy thousand *ḥūris* will welcome you, delighted to see you. Each one of them will have in their hand a brazier made of light spreading the fragrance of twig without fire. They will be wearing crowns fitted with gems from green jewels. They will hurry to your right side. When you part from your grave, Maryam daughter ᶜImrān will receive you with *ḥūrīs* like those with you. She will greet you and she and whoever is with her will begin the journey with you on your left side. Then your mother, the first believing woman in Allāh and His Messenger, Khadīja daughter of Khuwaylad will receive you and with her will be seventy thousand angels, holding banners of 'Allāh is the Greatest'.

[106] Muḥammad ibn al-ᶜAbbās reported on the authority of Muḥammad ibn Aḥmad ibn al-Hakam, on the authority of Muḥammad ibn Yūnus, on the authority of Ḥammād ibn ᶜĪsā, on the authority of al-Ṣādiq (AS), on the authority of his father (AS), on the authority of Jābir ibn ᶜAbd Allāh (RA) saying: The Messenger of Allāh (SA) entered the presence of Fāṭima (AS) while she was grinding the hand-mill, wearing a cloak made of camelhair. Therefore, when he looked at her, he cried and said, "O Fāṭima, have patience upon the bitterness of this world for the bounties of the hereafter." Thus, Allāh revealed to him: *And surely what comes after is better for you than that which has gone before. And soon will your Lord give you so that you shall be well-pleased. Biḥār al-Anwār*: vol. 16, pp 143, ch. 7, *ḥadīth* no. 9, and vol. 43, pp 85, ch. 4, & *Ta'wīl al-Āyāt al-Ẓāhirah*: pp 783, ch. 93, & *Tafsīr al-Ṣāfī* by Al-Fayḍ al-Kāshānī: vol. 5, pp 340, *ḥadīth* no. 5, & *Tafsīr Nūr al-Thaqlayn* by Al-Shaykh al-Ḥuwayzī: vol. 5, pp 594, *ḥadīth* no. 10, & *Manāqib Āli Abū Ṭālib* by Ibn Shahr Āshūb: vol. 3, pp 120, & *Tafsīr Majmᶜ al-Bayān* by Al-Shaykh al-Ṭabarsī: vol. 10, pp 382, & *Shawāhid al-Tanzīl*: vol. 2, pp 445, ch. 93, *ḥadīth* no. 1109-10, & *Tafsīr Thaᶜlibī* by Al-Thaᶜlibī: vol. 10, pp 225, & *Al-Durr al-Manthūr* by Jalāl al-Dīn al-Siyūṭī: vol. 6, pp 361, & *Fatḥ al-Qadīr* by Al-Shawkānī: vol. 5, pp 460, & *Tafsīr al-Ālwasī* by Ālwasī: vol. 30, pp 160, & *Manāqib ᶜAlī ibn Abū Ṭālib wa-Mā Nazala min-al-Qur'ān fī ᶜAlī* by Abū Bakr Aḥmad ibn Mūsā ibn Mardwayh al-Isfahānī: pp 199, *ḥadīth* no. 280.

[107] Qur'ān: 93: 5.

[108] It has been reported from Aḥmad ibn Mihrān (RA) who hurried and Aḥmad ibn Idrīs reported on the authority of Muḥammad ibn ᶜAbd al-Jabbār al-Shaybānī said: al-Qāsim ibn Muḥammad al-Rāzī related to me saying: ᶜAlī ibn Muḥammad al-Hirmazānī related to me on the authority of Abū ᶜAbd Allāh al-Ḥusayn ibn ᶜAlī (AS) saying: "When Fāṭima (AS) passed away, the Commander of the Faithful (AS) buried her secretly and hid the mark of her grave. Then he

stood up and turned to the grave of the Messenger of Allāh (SA) and said, "O Messenger of Allāh, peace be upon you from me and from your daughter who has come to you and who has hastened to meet you. O Messenger of Allāh, my patience regarding your chosen one has been exhausted, and my power of endurance has weakened, except that I have ground for consolation in having endured the great hardship and heartrending event of your separation. I laid you down in your grave when your last breath had passed (when your head was) between my neck and chest. Verily we are Allāh's and verily unto Him shall we return. Now the trust has been returned and what had been given has been taken back. As to my grief, it knows no bounds, and as to my nights, they will remain sleepless till Allāh chooses for me the house in which you are now residing.

Certainly, your daughter would apprise you of the joining together of your *Ummah* (people) for oppressing her. You ask her in detail and get all the news about the position. This has happened when a long time had not elapsed and your remembrance had not disappeared. My salutations [*salām*] be upon you both, the salutation of a grief-stricken and not a disgusted or hateful person; for if I go away, it is not because I am weary (of you), and if I stay it is not due to lack of belief in what Allāh has promised the endurers.

[109] Ibid.